Dodgers

Dodgers

JACKIE ROBINSON
PRO BALL'S FIRST BLACK STAR

By JAMES T. OLSEN

ILLUSTRATED by HAROLD HENRIKSEN

Library of Congress Number: 73-12437 ISBN: 0-87191-276-7

Published by Creative Education, Mankato, Minnesota 56001
Prepared for the Publisher by Educreative Systems, Inc.
Distributed by Childrens Press, 1224 West Van Buren Street, Chicago, Illinois 60607

Library of Congress Cataloging In Publication Data

James T. Olsen
Jackie Robinson; pro ball's first Black star
SUMMARY: A biography of the Negro whose distinguished baseball career inspired blacks everywhere and whose "cool" on the playing field helped open the door to other black athletes.
1. Robinson, John Roosevelt, 1919-1972—Juvenile literature. [1. Robinson, John Roosevelt, 1919-1972. 2. Baseball—Biography. 3. Negro athletes]
GV865.R6E38 796.357'092'4 [B] [92] 73-12437 ISBN 0-87191-276-7

There were tens of thousands of people lined up along the streets of Harlem and Bedford Stuyvesant. There was a marching line of people a mile long. One lady turned to the lady next to her and said: "We should be very proud of him He was the first black man to break into professional baseball." The other woman nodded and said: "He helped all of us, black and white."

A young man with tears in his eyes said: "We talked about him in school. The teacher said he meant history to black people."

"He meant history to all of us," his friend answered.

His grandfather had been a slave. His father had been a sharecropper in Georgia. And he had been a second baseman for the Dodgers. More than 25 years ago he made baseball history in Brooklyn, and now his coffin was returning there. At the age of 53, he died in Stamford, Connecticut. All the thousands of people were in a funeral procession. They were looking at the coffin of a hero who had died. His name was Jackie Robinson.

Jackie was the youngest child of Mallie and Jerry Robinson. On the last day of January in 1919, he was born in Cairo, Georgia, but he only lived there until he was eighteen months old. Mallie Robinson wanted the best for her children. She wanted them to have every chance to do well and have a good life. At that time the South was not the best place for them to get that chance. So Jackie and his sister and three brothers were taken to Pasadena, California. They grew up there with Mallie and their uncle.

Life in Pasadena was not easy for the Robinsons. Mrs. Robinson had to work as a maid cleaning other people's houses. She was not the only one who worked, though. Her children worked, too. From the time Jackie was a little boy, he helped his family out. He did all sorts of jobs. He delivered newspapers. He collected junk. He sold hot dogs at the sports events in the Rose Bowl. He did anything he could to help his family. Jackie didn't just watch games at the Rose Bowl, though. He played a few games himself.

"Jackie, we want a home run!" the kids would yell from the stands at John Muir Technical High School. Or they would yell, "Make a touchdown, Jackie!" or "Shoot a basket!" Jackie was very well known at school. He was a natural athlete. He starred in football, basketball, baseball, and track. He was following in the footsteps of his older brother, Mack. Mack had set a world's record for sprinting and was second only to Jessie Owens at the 1936 Olympic Games.

But Mack was not the only Robinson to set athletic records. In 1937, Jackie graduated from high school. He decided to go to Pasadena Junior College. Again he was a star. He set a record for the running

broad jump of 25 feet 6½ inches. He set a basketball record by making 28 points in one game, and he hadn't even played full time! In his second year of college he had the highest batting average of all the players in junior college: .466.

From junior college Jackie went to the University of California at Los Angeles. He went on an athletic scholarship to play football. And once again, Jackie made a name for himself. "Go, Jackie, Go!" the stands would yell. He averaged a 12 yard gain per carry. He led the country in yardage of punts returned. He was great in every sport: football, basketball, tennis, baseball, golf, track, and broad jumping. As Jackie's fellow students walked out of the stadium they would shake their heads and say, "He sure is great. I've never seen anything like him!"

Jackie's life didn't go as he had planned, though. He had to drop out of college in his junior year. His mother had become sick. His older brother had died, and his brother, Mack, had married. It was up to Jackie to take care of the family. But he found a way to help

his family without giving up sports. He got a job as an assistant athletic director at a camp. But once again Jackie's plans changed and he couldn't help his family for too long. In April, 1942, Jackie was drafted into

the Army.

While in the Army, Jackie learned a hard lesson about racial prejudice. He had refused to move to the back of a bus after he had been given orders to do so by a white officer. At that time blacks in many places in the United States were allowed to ride buses only if they went to the back of the bus. The front was only for white people. Jackie had lived in some places where this wasn't true and he didn't think anyone had the right to give such an order. He had been court martialed for that. The charges were finally dropped.

It was hard for blacks in America then. Even as an athlete. There was no place for them in professional sports—baseball, basketball, football. They could only play with other black athletes. They could not play with any white players because none of the clubs were integrated. And most of the people at that time thought it was a good thing. As one man said: "You know how fans look up to the players. Many of our fans are white people. They might become attached to a black home run hitter. Then where would we be?" Those might seem like strange words today, but not too long ago, that was the way most people felt.

Black players had to "stay with their own kind." The black teams were poor. They did not have much to offer their players. These players had to sleep in old and rundown hotels. Many times they had to eat in

places where they weren't even allowed to sit down because they were black. There were a few people who said that the blacks were "good enough to play in the big leagues," but still most people felt that the blacks should stay in their own leagues.

That was the kind of world Jackie Robinson lived in. Even though he was a great athlete, there wasn't any place for him. It looked as though Mallie Robinson's son would never get his chance.

But there was one white man who didn't go along with what people were saying. He was a very powerful white man. He was the president and manager of the Brooklyn Dodgers, and his name was Branch Rickey.

Rickey was a very smart man. He knew that the major ball clubs were hurting themselves by not letting the black athletes play. He knew that there were some very good black players, like Jackie Robinson. But Rickey also knew that it would be very hard to change the way people felt about black players in the major clubs. Prejudice would not die easily.

How to make the change happen? Rickey had to find men who were great ball players. They had to be strong men, but not just strong because they had a lot of muscles. Strong men who could bear up under insults from other players. Men who could stand the catcalls and jeers from the prejudiced crowds. These men would have to be tough. They would be paving the way for black players after them. These first players would be pioneers.

Rickey knew all of this. He knew he would have to find pioneer players. He knew that he would be a pioneer, too. Crazy? you say. You may be right, but that's the way things were at the time. It took hard work to change the way people felt about black players in pro ball.

Branch Rickey was a hard worker. And so was Jackie Robinson. Each man knew what he was up against. Rickey said: "I had to get a man who would carry the burden on the field. I needed a man who would carry the badge of martyrdom. The press had to accept him. He had to start a good reaction to the Negro race itself, for a bad reaction might have made the prejudice of other people even worse. And, I had to think about how the rest of the team would feel, too."

Rickey expected to have a hard time of it. His family was against the idea. His wife felt that he had done enough for baseball and that someone else should do this job. His friends were against him. Many blacks

thought that it would not work because of white prejudice. And most white people thought the whole idea was crazy. At the same time, Rickey would not give up on what he knew was right. He had thought it through carefully. He had been taught by his family from the time he was a young child to stick to what he believed. When he sent his scouts out to look for new, good ball players, he told them to be on the lookout for good black ball players because he wanted to bring them into his club.

There was a stack of scouting reports on Rickey's desk. Rickey sat there and slowly went through them. He saw one name again and again in the reports. The name was Jackie Robinson.

When Jackie was told about Rickey's interest in him, he said, "This may be a shot in the dark, but it could mean something for the future. Even if they don't pick me, they may at least see that there are Negro players around the country who should be given a

chance." Even then Jackie thought less about his own future than he did about the future of all good black athletes. All athletes, whether black or white, should have the chance to play pro ball.

Jackie knew about prejudice. But he was not afraid to stand up to it. His whole life up to this point had been part of the fight against prejudice. When he had been a ball player in college, he had told off the white sports writer who wouldn't even write about a black athlete. No matter how good he was. He had seen and felt racial prejudice from the time he had been born in the South. He had seen prejudice against blacks in housing, in employment, in recreational areas, in school, and even in the Armed Services.

Jackie was not afraid. He was outspoken, angry. And when he walked into the office of Branch Rickey on that bright Tuesday morning of August 28, 1945, he carried those feelings inside his heart and his head. When he saw Robinson, Rickey said to him: "Come in, come in." Jackie walked in proud and confident. The 63 year old Rickey picked up the stub of his cigar and started to puff on it. He looked at Robinson with his sharp eyes. Jackie sat there, his jaw strong, his shoulders broad, his handsome face.

"Do you know why you are here?" Rickey asked.

"Not really," Jackie answered.

"Well," Rickey began, "I want to bring you into the Brooklyn Dodgers. I have never seen you play, but my scouts have. They say you are a good ball player and I'll take their word for it."

Rickey then told Robinson what he would have to face as a black in pro ball. He told him he would have to take the insults. He would have to put up with all kinds of prejudice. Was he ready and willing to do that?

Jackie Robinson could take it. But Jackie wasn't happy about being insulted and not being able to fight back. He said that he wasn't a weak fellow. He was used to playing hard and tough. But he would try to keep his temper. Branch Rickey wanted more than that.

He wanted Jackie to give his word that he would not fight back. He wanted Jackie to stay silent to insult or attack. Unless Jackie was willing to "turn the other cheek" Rickey did not feel that he would give him a chance.

There it was, pure and simple. It was too much to ask of any man. Rickey knew it. So did Jackie Robinson.

"Can you do it?" Rickey asked. "Can you do it? Do you have the guts to play the game no matter what happens? Even out on the field? Base runners will slide towards you, spikes first. Pitchers will throw at your head. Men will call you names."

Jackie looked at Rickey for a moment. Then he answered with a smile, "Those things have been happening to me since I was born."

But Rickey would not give up. "Suppose I am a ball player and I slam into you at second base. When I get up, suppose I yell: 'You dirty black bum' . . . what do you do?"

Jackie answered, "Do you want a ball player who's afraid to fight back?"

"No," Rickey said. "I want a ball player with guts enough not to fight back. You've got to do this job with base hits and stolen bases and fielding ground balls. Nothing else."

Now Rickey swung his fist in the direction of Jackie's face. He once again asked him, "What do you do?"

Jackie whispered, "Turn the other cheek. Right?"

"That's right," Rickey answered quickly. "That's right."

And there it was. At that moment the two men had made their deal. Jackie was not to fight back. He was to play the best ball he could. But he was to stay 'cool' at all times. He was not to react to the insults,

threats, jokes that he knew would be part of his career in baseball. It was agreed at that meeting that there would be a three year contract and for that time Jackie was not to fight back. Rickey turned to him and said, "If we fail, no one will try it again for twenty years. We are dealing with the right of any American to play baseball—the American game."

Jackie was silent. He had made his deal. He knew that he would have to live up to it. And it would not be easy . . .

It wasn't. One day they put a black cat on the field and yelled, "Hey, Jackie, there's your brother!" The insults were so great that there were many times when Jackie couldn't sleep at night. He would hear those words and mean insults in his mind. He could hear the voices. He could see the hate and anger.

But he controlled himself. He kept his part of the bargain with Rickey. There were magazine articles about him, stories in the newspaper, personal interviews. Jackie knew that his own success was important for everybody, black and white. And he was sure that he would be successful: "Anybody who says I can't make it doesn't know what I've gone through to stay in the big leagues, and what I will go through." Jackie had broken through a seventy year old policy of keeping blacks out of baseball and he meant to see that the policy would be ended for all time.

Jackie was playing baseball that was really fine. It was a "personal triumph" in the words of one sports writer. Jackie surprised huge crowds with his ball playing. His batting ability, his tremendous speed, and his great fielding helped his teammates to play even better. He put on a show of playing baseball that excited both the fans and his own teammates. Those teammates who had first resented and suspected him grew to like and respect him because he was such a good ball player.

Many towns in the South would not allow "mixed athletics" in which black and white ball players played on the same field, to take place. The Dodgers would no longer play in these towns. They refused to play without Jackie. They respected him.

Crack! The baseball went soaring through the air. Right out of the ball park! Jackie ran around the

bases. The crowd screamed and yelled. They loved to watch Jackie play baseball. Since Jackie had joined the Dodgers, many more people were coming to their games. Many of them came just to see Jackie. His hitting, his running, his defensive play, and his teamwork were great, and so the fans came to watch. When Jackie played they sure got their money's worth.

There were sports writers who said "he is the best man on the bases that baseball knows today." In 1947, Jackie was named "Rookie of the Year" by Sporting News. Before the season closed, a "Jackie Robinson Day" was held at Ebbets Field. The Dodgers had won the National League Penant and more than any other person, Jackie Robinson had been the reason.

He certainly was the most daring base runner in the majors. In his first World Series (which the Dodgers lost 3-4) Jackie also played some really fine baseball. He was the runnerup in the sports writers' choice for first baseman on the Associated Press's make-believe All-Star baseball team. As Jackie put it, he was happy that he had had the chance to help the Negro race. For Jackie, baseball was the only way he could help the blacks.

In the meantime, Jackie started work on an autobiography of himself. He was working on a motion

picture, "Brooklyn, U.S.A." He worked with black youngsters "to help the boys." Jackie kept on fighting for civil rights in other areas than baseball. In 1955, Jackie moved his family and himself to Stamford, Connecticut which was almost all white. He explained his feelings at the time by saying that "our ultimate

desire is that our children have the same chances that white parents want for their children."

In 1956, Jackie Robinson finally traded in his spikes and left baseball for good. He was first a vice president for Chockfull O Nuts luncheonette chain. He helped to bring greater opportunities for jobs to blacks. Then a little later he left that company and went to work for Harlem's Freedom National Bank. At the same time, he was also helping John J. Rockefeller in New York to deal with some of New York's racial problems. But wherever he went his message was always the same: blacks want the same things for their children that whites do. The problem is to integrate the society by giving more chances to all minority peoples. Unless they too can have a chance for the American Dream and be an important part of it, there would be trouble. In his view, juvenile delinquency, crime and violence came out of conditions in the ghetto which made people angry. They felt left out and kept down. There was no way out and even if they left the ghetto, they were unwelcome in the world around them.

It is painful and sad that Jackie's son, Jackie Jr. followed part of the very life that his father had talked about and worked against. In 1964, by the time Jackie Jr. was 17 and a senior at Rippowam High School, he dropped out of school and signed up for the Army. He came home with wounds and a taste for drugs along with his Purple Heart. Shortly after he returned home, he was arrested and found with heroin. Finally, Jackie Jr. was able to kick his habit and he went to work for a group that helped other people kick the drug habit. On June 17, 1971, Jackie Jr. was in a car accident and was killed. The police report said that he had not been on drugs.

Perhaps Jackie Robinson Sr. was right when he said, "I guess I had more of an effect on other people's kids than I did on my own." He went on, "My problem was that I couldn't spend much time at home. I guess I thought that my family was secure . . . that we didn't have anything to worry about, so I went running around everywhere else." A reporter said that in fact, Jackie

had reached many other kids and Jackie only answered, "Well, I don't know. I find it pretty hard to see how I can reach other kids if I can't reach my own."

There was no question that Jackie had reached other kids. Jackie had reached America. That could be shown by the pioneering work that Jackie had done for blacks in pro sports. Now it is taken for granted that black athletes are an important part of American sports. That had not been true at the time Jackie had started in pro baseball. The "experiment" had worked because Jackie through hard work and courage had made it work. He had helped a whole movement that was not only true in sports but touched many other areas of American life.

As Jackie had seen it, that was the promise he had made to himself and Branch Rickey. He had kept his word. He worked at making a difference to his own people in the best way that he thought he could.

At his funeral, there was a man who had been forming people into a procession. The man complained that it was too much work and that he really hadn't wanted the job. Jackie Robinson had not felt that way. Nothing was ever too much work for him—whether it was trying to make a difference to kids, to baseball, or to his fellow blacks. Jackie was buried in Cypress Hills Cemetery, just a few miles from the site of the old Ebbets Field. As hard as so many people have tried,

how can you really sum up the man's life work? He was a man who saw the larger picture, the whole world around him. He saw what needed to be done and went ahead and did it.

The greatest thing that can happen to a baseball player is to be elected to the Baseball Hall of Fame. Jackie was given that honor in 1962. And the greatest

thing that can be said about any man is that he did his best to make the world around him better. That can be said about Jackie Robinson. For Jackie had done his work well for all of us. For his race was all men, not just black men, and he did a great deal for us all.

JACK NICKLAUS
BILL RUSSELL
MARK SPITZ
VINCE LOMBARDI
BILLIE JEAN KING
ROBERTO CLEMENTE
JOE NAMATH
BOBBY HULL
HANK AARON
JERRY WEST
TOM SEAVER
JACKIE ROBINSON
MUHAMMAD ALI
O. J. SIMPSON
JOHNNY BENCH
WILT CHAMBERLAIN
ARNOLD PALMER
A. J. FOYT
JOHNNY UNITAS
GORDIE HOWE

superstars! superstars! superstars!

CREATIVE EDUCATION SPORTS SUPERSTARS

WALT FRAZIER
PHIL AND TONY ESPOSITO
BOB GRIESE
FRANK ROBINSON
PANCHO GONZALES
LEE TREVINO
KAREEM ABDUL JABBAR
JEAN CLAUDE KILLY
EVONNE GOOLAGONG
ARTHUR ASHE
SECRETARIAT
ROGER STAUBACK
FRAN TARKENTON
BOBBY ORR
LARRY CSONKA
BILL WALTON
ALAN PAGE
PEGGY FLEMING
OLGA KORBUT
DON SCHULA
MICKEY MANTLE